RAP'

'N use the
# TSC communication forms
For use with the Term Service Contract

An NEC document

April 2013

---

### Construction Clients' Board endorsement of NEC3

The Construction Clients' Board recommends that public sector organisations use the NEC3 contracts when procuring construction. Standardising use of this comprehensive suite of contracts should help to deliver efficiencies across the public sector and promote behaviours in line with the principles of *Achieving Excellence in Construction*.

### Facilities Management Board support for NEC3

The Facilities Management Board recognises that the NEC Term Service Contracts support good practice in FM Procurement in the public sector.

**Cabinet Office UK**

BIFM recommends the use of NEC3 Term Service Contract and NEC3 Term Service Short Contract for all types of Facilities Management and maintenance contracts.

supported by

**BIFM**

ADVANCING OUR PROFESSION

neccontract.com

NEC is a division of Thomas Telford Ltd, which is a wholly owned subsidiary of the Institution of Civil Engineers (ICE), the owner and developer of the NEC.

The NEC is a family of standard contracts, each of which has these characteristics:

- Its use stimulates good management of the relationship between the two parties to the contract and, hence, of the work included in the contract.

- It can be used in a wide variety of commercial situations, for a wide variety of types of work and in any location.

- It is a clear and simple document – using language and a structure which are straightforward and easily understood.

NEC3 how to use the TSC communication forms is one of the NEC family and is consistent with all other NEC3 documents.

ISBN (complete box set) 978 0 7277 5867 5
ISBN (this document) 978 0 7277 5927 6
ISBN (Term Service Contract) 978 0 7277 5891 0
ISBN (Term Service Contract Guidance Notes) 978 0 7277 5921 4
ISBN (Term Service Contract Flow Charts) 978 0 7277 5923 8
ISBN (how to write the TSC Service Information) 978 0 7277 5925 2

British Library Cataloguing in Publication Data for this publication is available from the British Library.

Typeset by Academic + Technical, Bristol

Printed and bound in Great Britain by Bell & Bain Limited, Glasgow, UK

# CONTENTS

# FOREWORD

I was delighted to be asked to write the Foreword for the NEC3 Contracts.

I have followed the outstanding rise and success of NEC contracts for a number of years now, in particular during my tenure as the 146th President of the Institution of Civil Engineers, 2010/11.

In my position as UK Government's Chief Construction Adviser, I am working with Government and industry to ensure Britain's construction sector is equipped with the knowledge, skills and best practice it needs in its transition to a low carbon economy. I am promoting innovation in the sector, including in particular the use of Building Information Modelling (BIM) in public sector construction procurement; and the synergy and fit with the collaborative nature of NEC contracts is obvious. The Government's construction strategy is a very significant investment and NEC contracts will play an important role in setting high standards of contract preparation, management and the desirable behaviour of our industry.

In the UK, we are faced with having to deliver a 15–20 per cent reduction in the cost to the public sector of construction during the lifetime of this Parliament. Shifting mind-set, attitude and behaviour into best practice NEC processes will go a considerable way to achieving this.

Of course, NEC contracts are used successfully around the world in both public and private sector projects; this trend seems set to continue at an increasing pace. NEC contracts are, according to my good friend and NEC's creator Dr Martin Barnes CBE, about better management of projects. This is quite achievable and I encourage you to understand NEC contracts to the best you can and exploit the potential this offers us all.

**Peter Hansford**

**UK Government's Chief Construction Adviser**
**Cabinet Office**

# PREFACE

The NEC contracts are the only suite of standard contracts designed to facilitate and encourage good management of the projects on which they are used. The experience of using NEC contracts around the world is that they really make a difference. Previously, standard contracts were written mainly as legal documents best left in the desk drawer until costly and delaying problems had occurred and there were lengthy arguments about who was to blame.

The language of NEC contracts is clear and simple, and the procedures set out are all designed to stimulate good management. Foresighted collaboration between all the contributors to the project is the aim. The contracts set out how the interfaces between all the organisations involved will be managed – from the client through the designers and main contractors to all the many subcontractors and suppliers.

Versions of the NEC contract are specific to the work of professional service providers such as project managers and designers, to main contractors, to subcontractors and to suppliers. The wide range of situations covered by the contracts means that they do not need to be altered to suit any particular situation.

The NEC contracts are the first to deal specifically and effectively with management of the inevitable risks and uncertainties which are encountered to some extent on all projects. Management of the expected is easy, effective management of the unexpected draws fully on the collaborative approach inherent in the NEC contracts.

Most people working on projects using the NEC contracts for the first time are hugely impressed by the difference between the confrontational characteristics of traditional contracts and the teamwork engendered by the NEC. The NEC does not include specific provisions for dispute avoidance. They are not necessary. Collaborative management itself is designed to avoid disputes and it really works.

It is common for the final account for the work on a project to be settled at the time when the work is finished. The traditional long period of expensive professional work after completion to settle final payments just is not needed.

The NEC contracts are truly a massive change for the better for the industries in which they are used.

**Dr Martin Barnes CBE**

**Originator of the NEC contracts**

## ACKNOWLEDGEMENTS

The original NEC was designed and drafted by Dr Martin Barnes then of Coopers and Lybrand with the assistance of Professor J. G. Perry then of the University of Birmingham, T.W. Weddell then of Travers Morgan Management, T.H. Nicholson, Consultant to the Institution of Civil Engineers, A Norman then of the University of Manchester Institute of Science and Technology and P.A. Baird then Corporate Contracts Consultant, Eskom, South Africa.

NEC wishes to acknowledge and thank the *how to use TSC communication forms* project team for their input to this guidance.


The members of the Project team include:

  R. A. Gerrard, BSc(Hons), FRICS, FCIArb, FCInstCES
  P. Higgins, BSc, CEng, FICE, FCIArb

# Part 1 Introduction

NEC3 Contracts require various communications to be given. These might include an instruction, an acceptance or a notification, to name a few. These communications are threaded into the contract processes alongside the obligations of the various parties. For example, clause 22.1 of the NEC3 Term Service Contract (TSC) states

> **"The *Contractor* submits a revised plan to the *Service Manager* for acceptance..."**

This clause, read together with clause 21.1 obliges the *Contractor* at different times in the contract to produce a plan, to revise it and submit it for acceptance. The required communication in this clause takes the form of a submission of the revised plan by the *Contractor* to the *Service Manager*.

In turn, clause 22.1 states

> **"Within two weeks of the *Contractor* submitting a plan to him for acceptance, the *Service Manager* either accepts the plan or notifies the *Contractor* of his reasons for not accepting it."**

Here, the *Service Manager* has a certain time period to either accept the plan or notify his reasons for not accepting the plan. The communications here take the form of the *Service Manager* either be an accepting (the plan) or notifying (that he does not accept the plan, together with reasons).

TSC clause 13.1 details the communications the contract requires to be given, what form they take and what language writing should be in.

> **"Each instruction, certificate, submission, proposal, record, acceptance, notification, reply and other communication which this contract requires is communicated in a form which can be read, copied and recorded. Writing is in the *language of this contract*."**

As stated in the TSC Guidance Notes,[1] 'in a form that can be read, copied and recorded' includes a document sent by post, cable, electronic mail, facsimile transmission, and on disc, magnetic tape or other electronic means.

In contrast, the short contracts such as the NEC3 Term Service Short Contract (TSSC) requires

> **"Each communication which this contract requires has effect when it is received in writing at the last address notified by the recipient for receiving communications."**

The TSSC requires the correct communication to be given, such as notifications and acceptances, requires them to be in writing and details when these take effect.

On this basis, NEC produced a number of simple, basic forms for users to better manage their NEC3 Contracts. These do not cover all of the various communication forms that might be required, the intention being that forms for the likely frequent communications are provided but not for the infrequent communications. When using the TSC, *Service Manager*'s instructions to change the Service Information will occur more frequently than a *Contractor*'s proposal, for instance. The instruction form is provided, the proposal form is not but users can adapt those forms they have quite readily to other communication forms as and when required.

Forms are produced for most of the NEC3 Contracts, or can easily be adapted from others, except for the NEC3 Framework Contract and the NEC3 Adjudicator's Contract. Users can take the forms and adapt them to suit their projects as they see fit.

---

[1] NEC3 Term Service Contract Guidance Notes

Forms available for the NEC3 Term Service Contract (TSC) include:

- *Service Manager*'s instruction (SMI)
- *Service Manager*'s notification (SMN)
- *Contractor*'s notification (CN)
- Payment certificate (PC)
- Task Order (TO)

These are shown below.

---

**Service Manager's Instruction**

For use with TSC

To: _____          Date: _____

Service Name: _____          Service ID: _____

Instruction No: _____

---

Under clause _____ I instruct you to:

_____

_____

_____

_____

_____

_____

_____

_____

---

Copy to: _____

Signed: _____

For: _____          Date: _____

---

how to...

---

### *Service Manager*'s Notification
For use with TSC

To: _____          Date: _____

Service Name: _____          Service ID: _____

Notification No: _____

Under clause _____ I notify you:

_____

_____

_____

_____

_____

_____

_____

_____

Copy to: _____

Signed: _____

For: _____          Date: _____

---

| | Contractor's Notification |
|---|---|
| | For use with TSC |

To: _____   Date: _____

Service Name: _____   Service ID: _____

Notification No: _____

Under clause _____ I notify you:

_____

_____

_____

_____

_____

_____

_____

_____

Copy to: _____

Signed: _____

For: _____   Date: _____

**how to...**

**Payment Certificate**

For use with TSC

To: _____          Date: _____

Service Name: _____          Service ID: _____

Certificate No: _____

Under clause 51.1:

Prices for Services Provided to Date          £ _____

Plus other amounts to be paid to the *Contractor*          £ _____

Sub-total          £ _____

Less amounts to be paid by or retained from the *Contractor*          £ _____

Amount due          £ _____

Less amount due in the last payment certificate          £ _____

Sub-total          £ _____

Tax which the law requires the *Employer* to pay to the *Contractor*          £ _____

Change in the amount due since the last payment certificate which is certified for payment          £ _____

Copy to: _____

Signed: _____

For: _____          Date: _____

**Task Order**

For use with TSC Option X19

To: _____          Date: _____

Service Name: _____          Service ID: _____

Task Order No: _____

Further to our consultation, under Option X19 I instruct you to carry out the following Task:
[Include here a detailed description of the work in the Task]

_____

_____

_____

Priced list of items of work in the Task:
The following items are taken from the Price List

£ _____

£ _____

The following items have been assessed in the same way
as a compensation event

£ _____

£ _____

Total/forecast total of the Prices                £ _____

Task starting date: _____          Task completion date: _____

Amount of delay damages for the
late completion of the Task:          £ _____          per week/day

Copy to: _____

Signed: _____

For: _____          Date: _____

These simple NEC communication forms, together with Contract Datas for the NEC3
Contracts, are available as part of the membership of the NEC Users' Group (see

www.neccontract.com). Alternatively, these are provided to purchasers of digital NEC3 Contracts.

Users should note that some forms have multiple uses. For example, the *Contractor's* Notification form can be used to notify matters such as:

- a change of address for receiving communications (clause 13.2),
- early warnings (clause 16.1),
- compensation events (clause 61.3),
- failure of *Service Manager* in respect of compensation events (clause 61.4, 62.6, 64.3) and
- a dispute (clause W1.3(2)) or intention to refer to *tribunal* (clause W1.4(2) & (3)), (clause W2.4(2)).

Clause 13.7 states

> **"A notification which this contract requires is communicated separately from other communications."**

With the exception of notifications therefore, other communications could be communicated together.

The following parts of this guidance illustrate some completed forms applied to a fictitious project. This is a facilities management (FM) project based in New Zealand and uses the worked example of the TSC Contract Data from the TSC Guidance Notes. This is shown in Appendix 1. The associated example Price List is shown in Appendix 2.

It is usual to have a start-up meeting where matters such as communications protocol would likely feature. Who is going to act on behalf of the *Contractor* and to whom should communications be sent to? Is the address in Contract Data part two the one to be used for communications? Are there any delegates of the *Service Manager* on this project?

On our project, the *Service Manager* advised the *Contractor* he intended to delegate most of his duties and would notify the details to the Contractor, immediately following the start-up meeting. This was notified on SMN1 following discussions with the *Employer* as to the desired extent of delegation responsibilities.

---

*Service Manager's* **Notification**

To:      **Mrs Smith, NZ FM Contracting Ltd**     Date:     **1st May 2013**

Service Name:    **More Sustainability FM Services**     Service ID:   **1234**

Notification No: **1**

---

Under clause <u>14.2</u> I notify you:

that Mr J. Lomu is delegated all actions of the *Service Manager* in the contract except

the following clauses:

Clause 51

Clause 90–93

Option W1

His contact details are

---

Copy to: **Head Office**

Signed:

For:     **I C Consultants**                    Date: **1st May 2013**

---

# Part 2 Early warnings

Clause 16 deals with early warnings and is designed to be a reciprocal but simple risk management tool. If the *Contractor* or the *Service Manager* becomes aware of any of the matters stated in clause 16.1 they are obligated to notify an early warning.

> **"The *Contractor* and the *Service Manager* give an early warning by notifying the other as soon as either becomes aware of any matter which could..."**

The early warning process is entirely separate from the compensation event process. Sometimes matters start out as early warnings and may indeed become compensation events, but often not. When a compensation event arises, the *Service Manager* and *Contractor* are left only to deal with cost matters arising due to the event. When an early warning matter arises, the *Service Manager* and *Contractor* set about making and considering proposals for how the effect of the registered risks can be avoided and reduced, amongst other obligations, at risk reduction meetings.

There is little point and no obligation to notify an early warning of a matter which has happened and has no future consequence. The process is about seeking solutions to problems which is therefore to do with the future, not the past. If an event has happened it may well be a compensation event or perhaps a Defect, not something that requires an early warning to be notified.

In our project, the *Contractor* had been told by one of the *Employer*'s staff that most of the rooms would not be available at 1700hrs for cleaning purposes next month as there was an important project underway with staff likely working overtime. This starting time was stated in the Service Information. The *Contractor* considered this was a matter he was obliged to notify an early warning to the *Service Manager*. The communication is a notification and comes from the *Contractor* so the *Contractor*'s Notification form is used, as shown below.

---

*Contractor's* Notification

To: **Mrs I Certifier, I C Consultants**  Date: **3rd May 2013**

Service Name: **More Sustainability FM Services**  Service ID: **1234**

Notification No: **1**

Under clause 16.1 I notify you:

that Mr Jones of the *Employer's* staff has advised us that most rooms would not be

available next month at 1700hrs for cleaning, contrary to the availability stated in

the Service Information

Copy to: **Head Office**

Signed: *J.Smith*

For: **NZ FM Contracting Ltd**  Date: **3rd May 2013**

---

On receipt of this notified early warning, the *Service Manager* realised that she had not put together the first Risk Register and decided to compile this straight away, following the *Contractor's* notified early warning.

The first Risk Register contains all of the matters listed in Contract Data part one and two (shown in Appendix 1), together with the early warning notified by the *Contractor* earlier. The Risk Register is not a contract document, is not in place until after the contract is awarded and is a register that helps promote better management of risks which have not yet been avoided or reduced.

The Risk Register is defined in clause 11.2(14), the first part of the clause states where the risks come from:

> **"The Risk Register is a register of the risks which are listed in the Contract Data and the risks which the *Service Manager* or the *Contractor* has notified as an early warning matter."**

The second part of the clause states what must be shown on the register:

**"It includes a description of the risk and a description of the actions which are to be taken to avoid or reduce the risk."**

There is no Risk Register form produced by NEC, many organisations have their own procedures in place for such. This is fine but the parties need to ensure that the requirements of the contract are followed. The *Service Manager* included the two things stated above that the contract demands, but also added some additional column to suit the project. This is good management – regard the contract as a set of minimum obligations, there is nothing stopping the parties doing more than the minimum required if they feel it is in the interests of the project.

The *Service Manager* issued the Risk Register to the *Contractor* and instructed the *Contractor* to attend a risk reduction meeting to take place the next day.

| | | | | Risk Register |
|---|---|---|---|---|

To: **Mrs Smith, NZ FM Contracting Ltd**    Date: **6th May 2013**

Service Name: **More Sustainability FM Services**    Service ID: **1234**

Risk Register No: **1**

| ID | Source | Description of the risk | Description of the actions to be taken to avoid or reduce the risk | Now been avoided or have passed? |
|---|---|---|---|---|
| 1 | CD1 | Possible change of access security requirements during 2014 | | no |
| 2 | CD1 | Limited car parking availability for *Contractor*'s personnel | | no |
| 3 | CD1 | On-going lift replacement contract due to end December 2014 | | no |
| 4 | CD1 | On-site cafeteria to be separately refurbished during 2013 | | no |
| 5 | CD1 | Possible increase of *Employer*'s staff numbers by 20% during 2014 | | no |
| 6 | CD1 | Small extension to property commencing 2014 | | no |
| 7 | CD2 | Lack of local grounds maintenance expertise | | no |
| 8 | CD2 | Some catering requirements are seasonal | | no |
| 9 | CD2 | Short contract duration but considerable up-front investment required | | no |
| 10 | CN1 | Some rooms not available at 1700hrs | | no |

Copy to: **Head Office**

Signed:

For:    **I C Consultants**    Date: **6th May 2013**

The *Service Manager* and the *Contractor* attended the risk reduction meeting. Other people could have attended the meeting if either the *Service Manager* or *Contractor* considered this would be of benefit. This is detailed in clause 16.2.

At any risk reduction meeting, clause 16.3 requires

> **"those who attend co-operate in:**
>
> - **making and considering proposals for how the effect of the registered risks can be avoided or reduced,**
> - **seeking solutions that will bring advantage to all those who will be affected,**
> - **deciding on the actions which will be taken and who, in accordance with this contract, will take them and**
> - **deciding which risks have now been avoided or have passed and can be removed from the Risk Register."**

As shown, there are four basic requirements to work through in any risk reduction meeting. The meeting could last 5 minutes or 5 hours, there could be 2 people or 10, it could be in person, by teleconference or videoconference; the who, how, where, when aspects of the meeting are left to the *Service Manager* and *Contractor* to apply judgement in deciding what is best in the circumstances.

On our project, the attendees made their decision on CN1. As the *Contractor* would not start cleaning all rooms at 1700hrs, the *Contractor* would notify a compensation event each time he considered the right of access was denied. On balance, this would likely only last a month and was not considered to be a significant problem.

During the meeting they took the opportunity to address a few other matters listed on the Risk Register. These decisions were recorded, the Risk Register was revised and immediately issued to the *Contractor*.

| | | | | Risk Register |
|---|---|---|---|---|

**To: Mrs Smith, NZ FM Contracting Ltd**      Date: **7th May 2013**

Service Name: **More Sustainability FM Services**      Service ID: **1234**

Risk Register No: **2**

| ID | Source | Description of the risk | Description of the actions to be taken to avoid or reduce the risk | Now been avoided or have passed? |
|----|--------|--------------------------|-------------------------------------------------------------------|-----------------------------------|
| 1 | CD1 | Possible change of access security requirements during 2014 | | no |
| 2 | CD1 | Limited car parking availability for *Contractor*'s personnel | *Contractor*'s personnel will be encouraged to share lifts or get public transport (C) | yes |
| 3 | CD1 | On-going lift replacement contract due to end December 2014 | | no |
| 4 | CD1 | On-site cafeteria to be separately refurbished during 2013 | | no |
| 5 | CD1 | Possible increase of *Employer*'s staff numbers by 20% during 2014 | No longer a risk due to re-structuring (SM) | yes |
| 6 | CD1 | Small extension to property commencing 2014 | | no |
| 7 | CD2 | Lack of local grounds maintenance expertise | | no |
| 8 | CD2 | Some catering requirements are seasonal | | no |
| 9 | CD2 | Short contract duration but considerable up-front investment required | No action to be taken, *Contractor* has arranged for appropriate investment (C) | yes |
| 10 | CN1 | Some rooms not available at 1700hrs | Short term problem. Staff will be asked to vacate certain rooms by 1700hrs (SM) | no |

Copy to: **Head Office**

Signed:

For:     **I C Consultants**      Date: **7th May 2013**

This process continues throughout the contract period, early warnings are notified, captured on the Risk Register, risk reduction meetings are held and hopefully most problems are solved bringing advantage to all those who will be affected. The Risk Register is kept up-to-date through the risk reduction meetings and the parties can keep the risks in number ID order, or whether they have been avoided or passed, or by a most sophisticated likelihood/severity method, if they wanted to. There is no prescriptive requirement for such in the TSC, the parties can decide what is best for them.

# Part 3 The plan

Clauses 21 and 22 deal with the *Contractor*'s plan. Each plan is submitted to the *Service Manager* for acceptance, when this happens it becomes the Accepted Plan. Clause 11.2(1) states

> **"The Accepted Plan is the plan identified in the Contract Data or is the latest plan accepted by the *Service Manager*. The latest plan accepted by the *Service Manager* supersedes previous Accepted Plans."**

The plan must show all of the matters stated in clause 21.2 but there is no prescription format the plan itself takes. Quite commonly this might take the form of a Gantt chart with supporting documents, but it could be any number of visual and/or description documentation. The first plan might be identified in the Contract Data, established during the tender period, or if not then is submitted by the *Contractor* within the period stated in the Contract Data.

Within two weeks of the *Contractor* submitting a plan to the *Service Manager* for acceptance, clause 21.3 states the *Service Manager* either

> **"accepts the plan or notifies the *Contractor* of his reasons for not accepting it."**

The four stated reasons for the *Service Manager* to not accept the plan are stated in clause 21.3. When revised plans are submitted to the *Service Manager* for acceptance they should show the effects of implemented compensation events and other changes. The *Service Manager* again has to then accept or not accept in accordance with clause 21.3. Revised plans are submitted within the *period for reply* after the *Service Manager* has instructed the *Contractor* to, and when the *Contractor* chooses to (clause 22.1). The parties can react to the need to update the plan as they see fit for their project.

In addition to the clause 21/22 provisions for the plan itself, the plan features in a number of TSC processes:

- A Defect is "...a part of the *service* which is not in accordance with the applicable law or the **Accepted Plan**" (clause 11.2(4)).
- The *Service Manager*'s acceptance of a communication from the *Contractor* or of his work does not change the *Contractor*'s responsibility to Provide the Service or his liability for his **plan** or his design (clause 14.1).
- A reason for not accepting (the design of an item of Equipment) is that "...the design of the item will not allow the *Contractor* to Provide the Service in accordance with...the **Accepted Plan**..." (clause 23.1).
- The *Employer* allows the *Contractor* access to the Affected Property as shown on the **Accepted Plan** (clause 31.1).
- If no **plan** is identified in the Contract Data, one quarter of the Price for Services Provided to Date is retained in assessments of the amount due until the *Contractor* has submitted a first plan to the *Service Manager* for acceptance showing the information which this contract requires (clause 50.3).
- A compensation event is where "The *Service Manager* gives an instruction changing the Service Information except a change to the Service Information provided by the *Contractor* for his **plan** which is made either at his request or to comply with other Service Information provided by the *Employer* (clause 60.1(1)).
- Further compensation events are where:
  - The *Employer* does not provide the right of access to the Affected Property in accordance with the **Accepted Plan** (clause 60.1(2)).
  - The *Employer* does not provide something which he is to provide as stated in the Service Information in accordance with the **Accepted Plan** (clause 60.1(3)).
  - The *Employer* or Others do not work in accordance with the **Accepted Plan** or within the conditions stated in the Service Information (clause 60.1(5)).

- In any quotation for a compensation event, if "the **plan** for remaining work is altered by the compensation event, the *Contractor* includes the alterations to the **Accepted Plan** in his quotation" (clause 62.2).
- Assessments (of compensation events) are based upon the assumptions that the *Contractor* reacts competently and promptly to the compensation event, that any Defined Cost due to the event is reasonably incurred and that the **Accepted Plan** can be changed (clause 63.8).
- One of four instances the *Service Manager* assesses a compensation event is if "...when the *Contractor* submits quotations for a compensation event, he has not submitted a **plan** or alterations to a **plan** which this contract requires him to submit." (clause 64.1).
- The second of four instances is if "...when the *Contractor* submits quotations for a compensation event, the *Service Manager* has not accepted the *Contractor*'s latest **plan** for one of the reasons stated in this contract" (clause 64.1).
- The *Contractor* provides information which shows how each item description on the Price List relates to the operations on each **plan** which he submits for acceptance" (clause 21.4, Option A & C).
- If the *Contractor* changes a planned method of working at his discretion so that the item descriptions on the Price List do not relate to the operations on the **Accepted Plan**, he submits a revision of the Price List to the *Service Manager* for acceptance (clause 54.2, Option A & C). A reason for not accepting a revision of the Price List is that "...it does not comply with the **Accepted Plan** ..." (clause 54.3, Option A & C).
- The *Contractor* advises the *Service Manager* on the practical implications of the **Accepted Plan** and on subcontracting arrangements (clause 20.3, Option C & E).
- The *Contractor* changes his **plan** if it is necessary to do so in order to comply with the revised timetable (clause X12.3(7)).
- "The Service Information for the *Contractor*'s **plan** is in ..." (Contract Data part two).
- "The **plan** identified in the Contract Data is ..." (Contract Data part two).

There is no standard NEC form for a *Contractor*'s submission; this one is created using a template from one of the other forms.

---

|  | | **Contractor's Submission** |
| --- | --- | --- |
| To: | **Mrs I Certifier, I C Consultants** | Date: **1st May 2013** |
| Service Name: | **More Sustainability FM Services** | Service ID: **1234** |
| Submission No: **1** | | |

I submit the following under clause 21.1:

our first plan for acceptance (ref plan/1), as attached.

Copy to: **Head Office**

Signed: *J.Smith*

For: **NZ FM Contracting Ltd**          Date: **1st May 2013**

---

Clause 21.3 states

> **"Within two weeks of the *Contractor* submitting a plan to him for acceptance, the *Service Manager* either accepts the plan or notifies the *Contractor* of his reasons for not accepting it."**

On our project, the *Service Manager* was satisfied that all of the clause 21.2 requirements had been properly included in the plan, and then issued the following notification. If the *Service Manager* did not accept the plan, then he would notify the reason for not accepting – four reasons are given to the *Service Manager* in clause 21.3 for this.

There is no standard NEC form for a *Service Manager*'s acceptance; this one is created using a template from one of the other forms.

```
                                    Service Manager's Acceptance
  _____

  To:          Mrs Smith, NZ FM Contracting Ltd    Date:     3rd May 2013
  _____

  Service Name:   More Sustainability FM Services   Service ID:  1234
  _____

  Acceptance No: 1
  _____

  Under clause  21.3  I accept:

  your plan ref plan/1 dated 1st May 2013.
  _____
  _____
  _____
  _____
  _____
  _____
  _____
  _____

  Copy to: Head Office
  _____

  Signed:
  _____

  For:       I C Consultants                    Date: 3rd May 2013
```

# Part 4 Compensation events

Compensation events are events which, if they occur and do not arise from the *Contractor*'s fault, entitle the *Contractor* to be compensated for any effect the event may have on the Prices or completion of a Task ordered under a Task Order. A compensation event will often result in additional payment to the *Contractor* but may result in reduced payment.

Compensation events are listed in the core clauses. Further compensation events are stated in Options X2, X12 and X19 (the latter lists a further seven compensation events). The main list is in clause 60.1; this includes events (1) to (14).

There are four parts to the compensation event process within the TSC. These are notification, quotation, assessment and then implementation.

Most compensation events on most contracts will probably arise due to the *Service Manager* instructing a change to the Service Information. On our project, the *Employer* had some problems with the requirement in the Service Information to bulk buy special floor cleaning fluids. There was enough to last about a month and so the *Employer* asked the *Service Manager* to change the responsibility for providing this to the *Contractor*. The *Service Manager* immediately wrote the following instruction:

---

***Service Manager's* Instruction**

---

To:      **Mrs Smith, NZ FM Contracting Ltd**     Date:    **5th June 2013**

Service Name: **More Sustainability FM Services**     Service ID: **1234**

Instruction No: **1**

---

Under clause  14.3  I instruct you to:

procure the following special floor cleaning fluids as per the attached specification.

Part 14(b) of the Service Information is deleted.

---

Copy to: **Head Office**

Signed:

For:     **I C Consultants**                       Date: **5th June 2013**

---

Clause 61.1 requires the *Service Manager* to notify the *Contractor* of a compensation event at the time of giving the instruction. This is quite a novel requirement in standard forms of contract, most expect the *Contractor* to identify change; this reflects the good management required in the TSC.

The notification stage on our project occurs when, at the same time of issuing SMI1, the *Service Manager* notified this as a compensation event. Clause 13.7 requires that a notification which the contract requires is communicated separately from other communications:

---

| | | | |
|---|---|---|---|
| | | ***Service Manager*'s Notification** | |

| | | | |
|---|---|---|---|
| To: | **Mrs Smith, NZ FM Contracting Ltd** | Date: | **5th June 2013** |

| | | | |
|---|---|---|---|
| Service Name: | **More Sustainability FM Services** | Service ID: | **1234** |

Notification No: **2**

Under clause  61.1  I notify you:

that my instruction SMI1 is a compensation event under clause 60.1(1).

Copy to: **Head Office**

Signed:

For:     **I C Consultants**                                      Date: **5th June 2013**

After giving the instruction and notifying the compensation event, the *Service Manager* is required to instruct the *Contractor* to submit quotations, unless the event arises from a fault of the *Contractor* or quotations have already been submitted. This is stated in clause 61.1.

---

**Service Manager's Instruction**

---

To:          **Mrs Smith, NZ FM Contracting Ltd**      Date:      **5th June 2013**

---

Service Name:  **More Sustainability FM Services**         Service ID: **1234**

---

Instruction No: **2**

---

Under clause  61.1  I instruct you to:

submit a quotation for the compensation event that arises from SMI1.

---

Copy to: **Head Office**

Signed:

For:      **I C Consultants**                            Date: **5th June 2013**

---

The next stage of the compensation event process is the quotation; this is something for the *Contractor* to prepare and this comprises proposed changes to the Prices.

There are a number of provisions within the TSC that the *Contractor* and *Service Manager* need to be aware of during the preparation of the quotation. These include:

- Alternative quotations may be beneficial (see clause 62.1).
- The *Contractor* should submit details of his assessment with each quotation (see clause 62.2).
- If the plan for remaining work is altered by the compensation event, the *Contractor* includes the alterations to the Accepted Plan in his quotation (see clause 62.2).
- Whether the compensation event should be assessed in accordance with clause 63.1 or 63.2; or whether the *Service Manager* and *Contractor* agree to use rates and Prices in the Price List as the basis for assessment as clause 63.3.
- Whether the *Service Manager* has notified the *Contractor* of his decision that the *Contractor* did not give an early warning of a compensation event which an experienced contractor could have given (see clause 63.6).

---

                   © nec 2013 | neccontract.com

- Whether the quotation should make due allowance for any *Contractor*'s risk (see clause 63.7).
- If the compensation event is as a result of an instruction to change the Service Information in order to resolve an ambiguity or inconsistency (see clause 63.8).

Once these provisions are considered, the *Contractor* submits the quotation. Clause 62.3 states

> **"The *Contractor* submits quotations within three weeks of being instructed to do so by the *Service Manager*."**

---

|  |  |
|---|---|
|  | ***Contractor*'s Submission** |

| | | | |
|---|---|---|---|
| To: | **Mrs I Certifier, I C Consultants** | Date: | **12th June 2013** |
| Service Name: | **More Sustainability FM Services** | Service ID: **1234** | |
| Submission No: **2** | | | |

I submit the following under clause 62.3:

our quotation for SMI1 comprises the proposed change to the Prices of $500.00,

the details of our assessment is attached. Our plan for the remaining work is not

altered by this compensation event.

Copy to: **Head Office**

Signed: *J. Smith*

For: **NZ FM Contracting Ltd**          Date: **12th June 2013**

---

Clause 63.12 states that

> **"Assessments for changed Prices for compensation events are in the form of changes to the Price List."**

The changes to the Price List could result in items being modified, added or deleted. This particular compensation event resulted in an item being added to it. The *Contractor* can append the proposed changes to the quotation submission along with details of his assessment and any alterations to the Accepted Plan. As the Price List is quite small on this project, it is sensible to submit it as a whole, showing the changes. If it were multiple pages, then just stating or showing the proposed changes would be more appropriate. The same consideration is given to the Accepted Plan, where the contract only requires the alterations to be shown.

**Price List**

PART 1

| Item number | Description | Unit | Expected quantity | Rate ($) | Price ($) |
|---|---|---|---|---|---|
| 1 | Provide FM services as stated in SI 1.1 | months | 24 | 35,000 | 840,000 |
| 2 | Provide FM services as stated in SI 1.2 | weeks | 10 | 3,000 | 30,000 |
| 3 | Provide FM services as stated in SI 1.3 | sum | 1 | 5,000 | 5,000 |
| 4 | SMI1 – provide special floor cleaning fluids | sum | 1 | 500 | 500 |
| | | | The total of the Prices for Part 1 | | 875,000 |

Upon receipt of the quotation the *Service Manager*, in accordance with clause 62.3, can instruct the *Contractor* to submit a revised quotation (only after explaining his reasons for doing so), accept this or notify that he will be making his own assessment (which may happen in certain circumstances such as the *Contractor* not submitting a quotation and details of his assessment within the time allowed.

On our project, the *Service Manager* was happy with how the *Contractor* had assessed the quotation and acceptance of this (the details were not included here but assume they were assessed by the *Service Manager*).

---

**Service Manager's Notification**

To: **Mrs Smith, NZ FM Contracting Ltd**    Date:    **14th June 2013**

Service Name: **More Sustainability FM Services**    Service ID: **1234**

Notification No: **3**

---

Under clause 62.3 I notify you:

that I accept your quotation of $500.00 for the SMI1 compensation event.

---

Copy to: **Head Office**

Signed:

For:    **I C Consultants**    Date: **14th June 2013**

---

Clause 65.3 states

**"The changes to the Price List are included in the notification implementing a compensation event."**

The *Service Manager* could append the changed Price List to the notification implementing a compensation event.

**Price List**

PART 1

| Item number | Description | Unit | Expected quantity | Rate ($) | Price ($) |
|---|---|---|---|---|---|
| 1 | Provide FM services as stated in SI 1.1 | months | 24 | 35,000 | 840,000 |
| 2 | Provide FM services as stated in SI 1.2 | weeks | 10 | 3,000 | 30,000 |
| 3 | Provide FM services as stated in SI 1.3 | sum | 1 | 5,000 | 5,000 |
| 4 | SMI1 – provide special floor cleaning fluids | sum | 1 | 500 | 500 |
| | | | The total of the Prices for Part 1 | | 875,000 |

The final stage in the process is the implementation of the compensation event. This is not about implementing perhaps some additional *service* instructed, it is instead concerned with the closure of the compensation event itself and how this changes the Price List.

Clause 65.1 deals provides three instances when implementation takes place, in this part of our project it is the notification of the acceptance by the *Service Manager* of the *Contractor*'s quotation (first bullet). Clause 65.2 confirms the finality of the compensation event assessment, it is not to be revised if a forecast upon which it is based is shown by later recorded information to have been wrong.

The TSC comprises a series of selected clauses that need to be read together to make the whole. This can be demonstrated through the following sequence of clauses which get from the initial need to change the Service Information, to the payment for such:

- The *Contractor* Provides the Services in accordance with the Service Information (clause 20.1).
- The *Service Manager* may give an instruction to the *Contractor* which changes the Service Information (clause 14.3).
- The *Contractor* obeys an instruction which is in accordance with this contract and is given to him by the *Service Manager* (clause 27.3).
- The *Service Manager* giving an instruction changing the Service Information is a compensation event, with two stated exceptions (clause 60.1(1)).
- The compensation event is implemented when one of three instances occur (clause 65.1).
- Assessments for changed Prices for compensation events are in the form of changes to the Price List (clause 63.12).
- The changes to the Price List are included in the notification implementing a compensation event (Option A, clause 65.3).
- Information in the Price List is not Service Information (clause 54.1).
- The amount due includes the Price for Services Provided to Date (clause 50.2) which in turn is defined in Option A 11.2(17) as being the total of
  - the Price for each lump sum in the Price List which the *Contractor* has completed and
  - where a quantity is stated for an item in the Price List, an amount calculated by multiplying the quantity which the *Contractor* has completed by the rate.

For payment purposes on a TSC Option A contract in particular, it is preferable to reach agreement with compensation event assessments as quickly as the parties can as such events only fall for payment when they are both on the Price List and completed. This is different to the basis of payment for Options C and E.

# Part 5 Payment

The *Service Manager* is obliged to assess the amount due at each assessment date, as stated in clause 50.1. How the amount due is calculated is stated in clause 50.2, the *Service Manager* being obliged to consider any application for payment the *Contractor* has submitted on or before the assessment date, clause 50.4. The *Service Manager* certifies payment within one week of the assessment date.

There is nothing to stop the *Service Manager* and *Contractor* working together to jointly agree the amount due in accordance with the contract. On our project the parties did just that and the *Service Manager* issued the following payment certificate, with the *Employer* paying it by the latest date the contract stipulates. The *Contractor* confirmed to the *Service Manager* that the payment for all work carried out to date was subject to VAT at 20%. In accordance with 50.2, therefore, the *Service Manager* added 20% to the amount the *Employer* was required to pay.

**Payment Certificate**

To: **More Sustainability Ltd**　　　　Date: **1st June 2013**

Service Name: **More Sustainability FM Services**　　Service ID: **1234**

Certificate No: **1**

Under clause 51.1:

| | | |
|---|---|---|
| Prices for Services Provided to Date | $ | **40,000** |
| Plus other amounts to be paid to the *Contractor* | $ | **0** |
| Sub-total | $ | **40,000** |
| Less amounts to be paid by or retained from the *Contractor* | $ | **0** |
| Amount due | $ | **40,000** |
| Less amount due in the last payment certificate | $ | **0** |
| Sub-total | $ | **40,000** |
| Tax which the law requires the *Employer* to pay to the *Contractor* | $ | **6,000** |
| Change in the amount due since the last payment certificate which is certified for payment | $ | **46,000** |

Copy to: **Mrs Smith NZ FM Contracting Ltd**

Signed:

For:　**I C Consultants**　　　　Date: **1st June 2013**

Clause 50.4 requires the *Service Manager* to give the *Contractor*

> **"...details of how the amount due has been assessed."**

Clause 50.2 states that

> **"The amount due is**
>
> - **the Price for Services Provided to Date,**
> - **plus other amounts to be paid to the *Contractor*,**
> - **less amounts to be paid by or retained from the *Contractor*."**

In turn, the Price for Services Provided to Date in clause 11.2(17) for Option A states that it is

"...the total of

- the Price for each lump sum item in the Price List which the *Contractor* has completed and
- where a quantity is stated for an item in the Price List, an amount calculated by multiplying the quantity which the *Contractor* has completed by the rate."

On our project, there were no other amounts to be paid to the *Contractor*, such as X20 Key Performance Indicators for example. There were also no amounts to be paid by or retained from the *Contractor*, for example uncorrected Defects. At the first assessment date, it is just about how many of items on the Price List have been completed. These were as follows:

**Price List**

PART 1

| Item number | Description | Unit | Expected quantity | Rate ($) | Price ($) |
|---|---|---|---|---|---|
| 1 | Provide FM services as stated in SI 1.1 | months | 1 | 35,000 | 35,000 |
| 2 | Provide FM services as stated in SI 1.2 | weeks | 0 | 3,000 | 0 |
| 3 | Provide FM services as stated in SI 1.3 | sum | 1 | 5,000 | 5,000 |
| | | | The total of the Prices for Part 1 | | 40,000 |

# Part 6 Task Orders

Task Orders become a part of the contract if Option X19 is incorporated in the Contract Data part one first bullet. Task Orders provide a way of creating mini-projects within the life of the TSC. A Task Order is defined in Clause X19.1(2) as

> "...the *Service Manager*'s instruction to carry out a Task"

and a Task is defined in clause X19.1(1) as

> "...work within the *service* which the *Service Manager* may instruct the *Contractor* to carry out within a stated period of time".

Clause X19.2 requires the *Service Manager* to consult with the *Contractor* about the contents of a Task Order before he issues it.

On our project, the *Employer* asked the *Service Manager* about adding to some of the *service* that the *Contractor* provides. As the *Employer* wanted the additional *services* started and finished within a quite short space of time, the *Service Manager* decided it was best to introduce this as a Task Order and get this done over a weekend, which is something not provided for in the Service Information. Clause X19.3 provides that the Prices for items in the Task price list which are not taken from the Price List are assessed in the same way as for compensation events. The additional weekend work costs the *Contractor* would incur would therefore be dealt with as a compensation event. The *Service Manager* consulted with the *Contractor* straight away and the following was agreed:

---

**Task Order**

---

To: **Mrs Smith, NZ FM Contracting Ltd**   Date: **5th November 2013**

Service Name: **More Sustainability FM Services**   Service ID:   **1234**

Task Order No: **1**

---

Further to our consultation, under Option X19 you are instructed to carry out the following Task:

Paint the 3 rooms marked A, B & C on the attached sketch, using type 1 paint

specification as described in Service Information, to be carried out the weekend

of 23rd and 24th November 2013.


Priced list of items of work in the Task:
The following items are taken from the Price List

Paint room type A, 1 nr @ $200.00                                    $   **200.00**

Paint room type B, 2 nr @ $300.00                                    $   **600.00**

The following items have been assessed in the same way
as a compensation event


Weekend work costs (details attached)                                $   **220.00**

Total/~~forecast total~~ of the Prices                               | $ **1,020.00** |

Task starting date: **23rd November 2013**        Task completion date: **24th November 2013**

Amount of delay damages for the
late completion of the Task:        $  **Nil**   per week/~~day~~

---

Copy to: **Head Office**

Signed: _(signature)_

For:     **I C Consultants**                          Date: **5th November 2013**

---

     © nec 2013 | neccontract.com

Clause X19.2 states

**"When a Task Order is issued**

- **the priced list of items for the Task is inserted in the Price List, and**
- **the work involved is added to the Service Information."**

This clause goes on to state that

**"An instruction to carry out a Task is not a compensation event."**

The Price List on our project would change as follows, only Part 1 is shown, Part 2 is a list of *services* the *Employer* expects to need and will ask the *Contractor* to provide.

## Price List

PART 1

| Item number | Description | Unit | Expected quantity | Rate ($) | Price ($) |
|---|---|---|---|---|---|
| 1 | Provide FM services as stated in SI 1.1 | months | 24 | 35,000 | 840,000 |
| 2 | Provide FM services as stated in SI 1.2 | weeks | 10 | 3,000 | 30,000 |
| 3 | Provide FM services as stated in SI 1.3 | sum | 1 | 5,000 | 5,000 |
| **Compensation events** | | | | | |
| 4 | SMI1 – provide special floor cleaning fluids | sum | 1 | 500 | 500 |
| **Task Orders** | | | | | |
| No. 1 | Paint room type A | nr | 1 | 200 | 200 |
| No. 1 | Paint room type B | | 2 | 300 | 600 |
| No. 1 | Weekend work costs | sum | | 220 | 220 |
| | | | The total of the Prices for Part 1 | | 876,550 |

This updated Price List allows for the changes to be considered when assessing the amount due at each assessment date. There could be a series of Task Orders issued during the term of the contract, or the *Service Manager* might simply instruct changes to the Service Information. The only difference is that Task Orders has the completion date fixed and allowance could be made for delay damages. The *Service Manager* can use whichever route he considers is best in the circumstances, ideally talking these through with the *Contractor* first if they haven't already formed the subject of an early warning.

# Part 7 Defects

There is a reciprocal obligation on both the *Service Manager* and *Contractor* to notify each other of each Defect 'as soon as' they find one. This is as stated in clause 42.1. The definition of a Defect is stated in clause 11.2(4) which states

**"A Defect is**

- **a part of the *service* which is not provided in accordance with the Service Information or**
- **a part of the *service* which is not in accordance with the applicable law or the Accepted Plan."**

Clause 42.1 goes on to state

**"The *Contractor* corrects a Defect whether or not the *Service Manager* notifies him of it."**

On our project, the *Contractor* notified the *Service Manager* of the following Defect:

---

|  |  |
|---|---|
|  | ***Contractor*'s Notification** |

To: **Mrs I Certifier, I C Consultants**     Date: **3rd June 2013**

Service Name: **More Sustainability FM Services**     Service ID: **1234**

Notification No: **2**

Under clause  42.1  you are notified:

We have cleaned the windows externally and these do not meet the requirements of

Service Information part B-123. We have arranged for these to be re-done

tomorrow. We will look again at our method of cleaning the windows and let you

have our considerations shortly, probably revising our plan.

Copy to: **Head Office**

Signed: *J.Smith*

For: **NZ FM Contracting Ltd**     Date: **3rd June 2013**

---

Clause 42.2 states that it is for the *Contractor* to

**"...correct notified Defects within a time which minimises the adverse effect on the *Employer* or Others."**

In the *Contractor*'s notification, one imagines that the proposed time to correct the notified Defect was acceptable and the *Service Manager* did arrange for the *Employer* to allow the *Contractor* access to correct the Defect. If the *Contractor* does not correct a Defect within the time required by the contract then clauses 42.2 states it is for the *Service Manager* to assess

**"...the cost to the *Employer* of having the Defect corrected by other people and the *Contractor* pays this amount."**

These are provisions to deal with uncorrected Defects as above or alternatively there could be a proposal by either the *Contractor* or *Service Manager* to accept the Defect, which would lead to revised Prices. This is dealt with in clause 43. The Defect process is quite a simple one involving notification then a choice of correcting the Defect, dealing with the financial consequence of an uncorrected Defect or accepting the Defect.

# Part 8  Managing communications

In the Introduction to this guide it states 'NEC3 Contracts require various communications to be given'. These can be both various and sometimes quite extensive. Consider a TSC Option A contract with a well written Service Information, minimal instructed change to it and minimal problems that arise through the early warning process. In this case, the number of communications might be quite minimal. Contrast this with a TSC Option E with a developing Service Information undergoing constantly instructed change, along with considerable problems that arise through the early warning process. Here, the number of communications could be quite extensive.

Users will therefore need to consider a number of factors when deciding the communication system that is appropriate for their needs. On a TSC contract, the following should be considered:

- Which main Option is it and what would be the communication implications of each?
- How clearly defined is the Service Information, what degree of change to this is likely?
- Do the *Employer/Contractor/Service Manager* already have appropriate systems in place?
- What is the extent of risks acting on the project?

This consideration will help shape the appropriate communication system for the project, which could range from a manual based system, using the simple NEC3 contract communication forms used in this guide, through to one of a number of technology based process systems available to users.  More details on the technology systems can be found on www.neccontract.com . If the manual based system, then consider putting together a schedule to record and reconcile communications. This would ensure the simple consecutive numbering system is correctly maintained as well as link different communications related to the same subject.

To finish, below are a few useful tips for users to help comply with the TSC requirements for communications:

- Follow the processes carefully – use 'notify', 'accept', 'instruct' etc as the particular clause requires.
- Decide if a manual system or technology based system is best for the project.
- If manual system, agree whether the simple NEC communication forms will be used, add to them if needed, create others if needed; fill in the repetitive data; decide on a tracker schedule.
- If technology based system, which one is best for your particular requirements?
- Finally and when completing the communication forms, use the language of the contract, present tense, plain English.

# Appendix 1 Contract Data

## CONTRACT DATA
### Part one – Data provided by the *Employer*

### 1 GENERAL

- The *conditions of contract* are the core clauses and the clauses for main Option **A**, dispute resolution Option **W1** and secondary Options **X2, X17, X18, X19, X20 and Z** of the NEC3 Term Service Contract April 2013.

- The *service* is **providing facilities management services to the head office of More Sustainability Ltd in Christchurch, New Zealand.**

- The *Employer* is

  Name     **More Sustainability Ltd**

  Address   **Eco Road, Christchurch, New Zealand. Tel +64 (03-333 3333)**

- The *Service Manager* is

  Name     **Mrs I Certifier**

  Address   **I C Consultants, Bridge Road, Christchurch, New Zealand.**

- The *Adjudicator* is

  Name     _____

  Address   _____

- The Affected Property is **the head office of More Sustainability Ltd in Christchurch, New Zealand including the car parking and adjacent landscaping areas.**

- The Service Information is in **document ref FM/Gen1.**

- The *language of this contract* is **English**.

- The *law of the contract* is the law of **New Zealand**.

- The *period for reply* is **two** weeks.

- The *Adjudicator nominating body* is the **Building Disputes Tribunal NZ Ltd**.

- The *tribunal* is **litigation**.

- The following matters will be included in the Risk Register

**Possible change of access security requirements during 2014**

**Limited car parking availability for *Contractor*'s personnel**

**On-going lift replacement contract due to end December 2014**

**On-site cafeteria to be separately refurbished during 2013**

**Possible increase of *Employer*'s staff numbers by 20% during 2014**

**Small extension to property commencing 2014.**

## 2 THE *CONTRACTOR*'S MAIN RESPONSIBILITIES

- The *Contractor* prepares forecasts of the final total of the Prices for the whole of the *service* at intervals no longer than **monthly**.

## 3 TIME

- *The starting date* is **1st May 2013**.
- *The service period* is **2 years**.

## 5 PAYMENT

- The *assessment interval* is **monthly**.
- The *currency of this contract* is the **New Zealand dollar**.
- The *interest rate* is **4** % per annum above the **base lending** rate of the **Reserve Bank of New Zealand**.
- The period within which payments are made is **one week**.

## 8 RISKS AND INSURANCE

- The minimum amount of cover for insurance against loss of or damage caused by the *Contractor* to the *Employer*'s property is **$1,000,000 (one million dollars)**.
- The minimum amount of cover for insurance in respect of loss of or damage to property (except the *Employer*'s property, Plant and Materials and Equipment) and liability for bodily injury to or death of a person (not an employee of the *Contractor*) arising from or in connection with the *Contractor*'s Providing the Service for any one event is **$10,000,000 (ten million dollars)**.
- The minimum limit of indemnity for insurance in respect of death of or bodily injury to employees of the *Contractor* arising out of and in the course of their employment in connection with this contract for any one event is **$10,000,000 (ten million dollars)**.
- The insurance against loss of or damage to Plant and Materials is to include cover for Plant and Materials provided by the *Employer* for an amount of **$50,000 (fifty thousand dollars)**.

## Option W1

- The *arbitration procedure* is **the latest version of the Institution of Civil Engineers of the United Kingdom Arbitration Procedure or any amendment or modification to it in force when the arbitrator is appointed**.
- The place where the arbitration is to be held is **Auckland**.
- The person or organisation who will choose an arbitrator
    - if the Parties cannot agree a choice or
    - if the *arbitration procedure* does not state who selects an arbitrator is **the Institution of Civil Engineers of the United Kingdom**.

## Option X17

- The *service level table* is in document **SLT1**.

## Option X18

- The *Contractor*'s liability to the *Employer* for indirect or consequential loss is limited to **$250,000 (two hundred and fifty thousand dollars)**.
- For any one event, the *Contractor*'s liability to the *Employer* for loss of or damage to the *Employer's* property is limited to **$1,000,000 (one million dollars)**.
- The *Contractor*'s liability for Defects due to his design of an item of Equipment is limited to **$100,000 (one hundred thousand dollars)**.
- The *Contractor*'s total liability to the *Employer* for all matters arising under or in connection with this contract, other than the excluded matters, is limited to **$500,000 (five hundred thousand dollars)**.
- The *end of liability date* is **6** years after the end of the *service period*.

## Option X19

- The *Contractor* submits a Task Order programme to the *Service Manager* within **5** days of receiving the Task Order.

## Option X20

- The *incentive schedule* for Key Performance Indicators is in document **IS1**.
- A report of performance against each Key Performance Indicator is provided at intervals of **3** months.

## Option Z

- The *additional conditions of contract* are **in document reference ACoC1.**

## Part two – Data provided by the *Contractor*

- The *Contractor* is

  Name  **NZ FM Contracting Ltd**.

  Address  **The Hollow, Christchurch, New Zealand. Tel +64 (03-321 3909)**

- The *direct fee percentage* is **13** %.

- The *subcontracted fee percentage* is **13** %.

- The key people are

(1) Name  **Mrs Smith**

   Job  **FM Manager**

   Responsibilities  **Manage the day to day running of the contract**

   Qualifications  **as attached CV**

   Experience **as attached CV**.

(2) Name  **Mr John Clean**

   Job  **Contracts Director**

   Responsibilities  **Overall responsibility for successful delivery of FM services on the contract**

   Qualifications  **as attached CV**

   Experience  **as attached CV**.

- The following matters will be included in the Risk Register

  **Lack of local grounds maintenance expertise**

  **Some catering requirements are seasonal**

  **Short contract duration but considerable up-front investment required.**

- The plan identified in the Contract Data is **reference FM/plan/1**.

- The *price list* is attached in **PL1**.

- The tendered total of the Prices is **$875,000 (eight hundred and seventy five thousand dollars)**.

# Appendix 2 Price List

The Price List is in two parts. Part 1 is for work described in the Service Information not requiring the *Service Manager* to issue a Task Order. Part 2 is for work to be carried out within a stated period of time on a Task by Task basis and instructed by Task Order. The *service* may comprise work under Part 1 only or Part 2 only or a mix of both.

The rates and Prices entered for each item includes for all work and other things necessary to complete the item.

**Price List**

PART 1

| Item number | Description | Unit | Expected quantity | Rate ($) | Price ($) |
|---|---|---|---|---|---|
| 1 | Provide FM services as stated in SI 1.1 | months | 24 | 35,000 | 840,000 |
| 2 | Provide FM services as stated in SI 1.2 | weeks | 10 | 3,000 | 30,000 |
| 3 | Provide FM services as stated in SI 1.3 | sum | 1 | 5,000 | 5,000 |
| | | | The total of the Prices for Part 1 | | 875,000 |

PART 2

| Item number | Description | Unit | Expected quantity | Rate ($) | Price ($) |
|---|---|---|---|---|---|
| 1 | Replace windows <2 m$^2$ in area | nr | 4 | 500 | 2,000 |
| 2 | Replace windows >2 m$^2$ in area | nr | 4 | 750 | 3,000 |
| 3 | Replace guttering | m | 50 | 20 | 1,000 |
| 4 | Replace door locks | sum | 1 | 1,000 | 1,000 |
| 5 | Replace fridge type 1 | nr | 1 | 1,000 | 1,000 |
| 6 | Replace carpet type 1 | m$^2$ | 100 | 50 | 5,000 |
| 7 | Replace window blinds | sum | 1 | 2,000 | 2,000 |
| 8 | Paint room type A | nr | 5 | 200 | 1,000 |
| 9 | Paint room type B | nr | 5 | 300 | 1,500 |
| | | | The total of the Prices for Part 2 | | 17,500 |